The fruit of the Spirit for everyday life!

John Coleman

I0159492

for Teachers, Catechists, Parents and Seekers

Dedicated to Clint.
Whatever Clint tackled in life he tackled with passion.
This has always been an inspiration for me.
Thanks big bro.

AUTHOR'S NOTE

This simple program, based on the fruit of the Spirit (Galatians 5:22), is just that: a simple (yet profound) program when woven into one's daily life. The idea may be carried internally; continuously putting it into practice. With intention (on a fruit), desire and action one's life can change. I hope yours does too! May the 'Spirit within' manifest its passionate love by leading you to a deeper contentment and peace.

The fruit of the Spirit is really one (ninefold) fruit. These are the 9 fruits that all Christians (indeed all 'good' people) should be developing in their lives. For ease of grammatical structure I have chosen to use the term 'fruits of the Spirit' in the body of the text.

A sincere thank you goes to Sr Marie Townsend SN and Dr Jennifer Gardner for their critical reading, guidance and suggestions. Thanks to Rev. Michael Leek osb for his reading and input.

Thanks also to Maria Rohr, a woman of boundless energy, for putting out the challenge which resulted in this simple idea finally being put to paper. I am also grateful to Spectrum Publications.

Finally, I wish to thank my wife, Shelley. Her love, support and wise questioning helped to 'sharpen this sword'.

First published in Australia in 2011
By Spectrum Publications Pty Ltd
PO Box 75, Richmond, Vic Australia 3121
Telephone: (+61) 1300 540 736
Facsimile: (+61) 1300 540 737
email: spectrum@spectrumpublications.com.au
web: www.spectrumpublications.com.au

Cover Design: xy arts
Typesetting by Spectrum Publications PL

Typeface: Arial / Sand

ISBN: 978-0-86786-218-8 (Standard paperback)

Notes:
Thomas Green sj, Opening to Prayer, Ave Maria Press, 1977.
The Jerusalem Bible (Popular Edition), Darton Longman & Todd, London, 1968.

WHAT IS THE PURPOSE OF THIS LITTLE BOOK?

The aim of this little book is to give teachers, catechists, parents and others a simple yet meaningful approach to teaching young people about the fruits of the Spirit as cited in Galatians 5:22. This approach offers clear values to assist and enrich the lives of our young people. Such a way of being may enable them to become the best people they can be. The book helps us to understand that the fruits of the Spirit are not just something we learn at a Confirmation class and promptly forget. Rather, the fruits of the Spirit are growing and deepening in our lives *from our Baptism (Christening)* **and can be a lifelong exploration**. The book offers a concrete guide outlining how they may be introduced to students and young people. In his book called 'Opening to God', Thomas Green sj speaks of the nine fruit of the Spirit as touchstones of a true life of prayer. They provide a clear guide post or way of being for the Christian journey or for genuine seekers.

Workshop available
A workshop presentation for adults is available which includes an understanding (theology) of why the fruits of the Spirit are considered important. For further information contact:
fruit@spectrumpublications.com.au

This little book seeks to complement the workshop or it may be used independently.

A Thought:
The fruit of the Spirit (Galatians 5:22)

With the gift of our Baptism (and the sacrament of Confirmation) each of us is called to live and grow in the nine fruit of the Spirit. (Gal. 5:22)

As we live out the gifts of our Baptism and Confirmation we strive to allow the Spirit (dwelling within) to manifest itself in our daily lives. This may be evidenced through our personal growth in:
love, peace, joy, kindness, patience, trustfulness, self control, goodness, and gentleness.

However, within our humanity we are challenged and do not always live out these fruits of the Spirit as we might desire. In fact, we often fall short!

A Goal:
Our growth, as fully initiated Christians, may be reflected in the continued growth and manifestation of the fruits of the Spirit in our everyday lives.

CONTENT

INTRODUCTION

Whether you are a teacher, a catechist, a parent or a seeker wishing to give those young ones in your care a template or a pathway for leading a good and wholesome life, this little book is for you. Within these pages is an approach we may use to deepen our own and a young person's understanding and appreciation of the fruits of the Spirit for daily living.

The fruits of the Spirit, rather than simply being something one learns during a Confirmation preparation class and promptly forgets, offer a life-long journey of exploration. In a sense, they can be a measuring stick for each of us as we strive to become 'better people' on the journey of life.

As people of the Spirit we are invited to become people of:

Love, Peace, Joy, Kindness, Patience, Trustfulness, Self Control, Gentleness, Goodness. (Galatians 5:22)

The fruits of the Spirit are a tangible template for Christians, seekers, indeed, all human beings to grow as better people.

CHAPTER ONE
An Awakening (How it all Began)

Every now and again we seem to take a 'leap forward' in our understanding of life. Understanding the real nature of the fruits of the Spirit (Gal. 5:22) is one such way of taking a major leap in appreciating life's purpose and meaning.

This story began some thirty years ago on a simple bus journey from the countryside to the cityscape. A gem of a gift was about to unfold – ever so slowly.

The Bus Trip:

She sat in the front seat of the bus. Her large, white-brimmed hat and loose long-flowing colourful dress ensured she created a presence. **She** became the focus as the bus wended its way through the tall timbers and vivid green pastures of the Upper Yarra Valley (Victoria, Australia) carrying all three passengers. The bus would take us as far as the train station. From there the train would convey us on the final part of our journey into the suburbs and city.

As the bus continued its journey, the lady in the wide-brimmed hat and long-flowing dress began to sing aloud. She had a glorious voice. She sang song after song. What a joy! The performance was worthy of a costly concert in some well-named stadium around the world. This was a pure gift and a pleasure.

As we alighted from the bus, making our way to the train station ticket booth, the casual remark, 'Thank you. That is a beautiful gift you have,' drew the immediate response.
'You're a Christian. Aren't you?' It felt like *the questioning accusation of the maid to Peter the night before Jesus died, 'aren't you one of his followers?'*
Somewhat taken aback it took a moment to accept and acknowledge that the observation was correct.

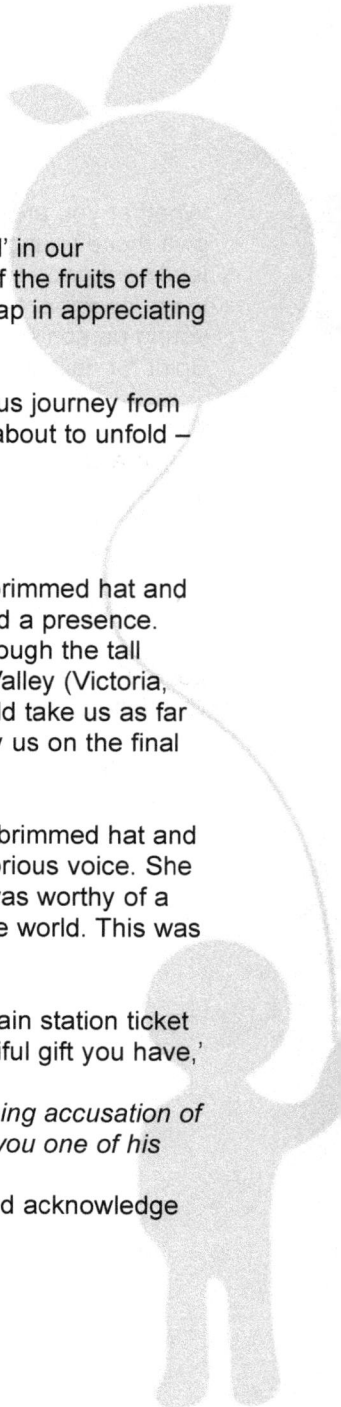

'Yes,' came the still somewhat surprised response.
'Do you know how I could tell?' she barked back with confidence.
'No.'
'Everyone tells me I have a lovely voice. But you used the word gift.' Somewhat stunned by the exchange, head down, I made my way to the ticket booth. With ticket firmly in hand a seat was the next decision. No sooner had this been done when in the aisle beside me stood the lady with the big white hat and long-flowing dress. She promptly sat beside me.

The train began its journey and the conversation continued. For the whole of the journey she talked about the presence of Jesus in one's life in its various forms. What may soon sound somewhat negative was actually the beginning of one of the greatest gifts received. The irony of receiving this gift is that I shall never be able to thank the giver. She was unknown to me. She appeared in and then disappeared from my life. But the seed had been planted. She was the messenger. She had played her part to perfection then simply vanished from the stage. So the conversation went on.

The further the train journey went, the more it seemed that Jesus was 'shoved down my throat'. Do not get me wrong. She clearly loved and believed in the message of Jesus. But something did not sit right for me.

For three days I walked around my workplace disturbed by the experience. For three days, I could not name this disturbance. She clearly loved the Lord, but the manner in which she shared this message left me feeling deeply disturbed. I pondered. *Something did not feel right.*

On the third day the moment of revelation dawned. There was no gentleness in the manner with which she conveyed the message. Gentleness! There was no gentleness in the manner of sharing her good news. How the leap was made from this moment of dawning to Galatians 5:22 (Christian Scriptures – where Paul names the fruits of the Spirit) is lost in time. But there, before my eyes, were the words…

> *What the Spirit brings is different; love, joy, peace, patience, kindness, goodness, trustfulness, gentleness and self-control. There can be no law against things like that, of course.*
> *(Galatians 5:22-23)*

What seemed like a mountain of not knowing or searching for 'the more' in life had been split asunder. The pathway, true and sure had revealed itself. The key had been handed over. It was simply now to begin the journey through the mountain pass to the vista waiting beyond. The next part of the journey of life had begun.

CHAPTER TWO
Understanding the fruit of the Spirit

As Christians or seekers, we receive the gift of the Spirit (Holy Spirit) at Baptism (Christening). The fruits of the Spirit are a tangible way of expressing our inner growth as Christians or simply as people who are seekers for 'the more' in life.

If we are truly growing interiorly as people, as Christians or genuine seekers, then we shall be growing in the fruits of the Spirit. The fruits of the Spirit will be evidenced in our daily lives.

Like anything else of value, the fruits of the Spirit take time to grow. It takes time for us to change. There is a need to practise, to be patient and to persevere for this change to occur within. Anything of real value usually takes time. So, be patient. Keep focussing on the fruits of the Spirit in which we wish to grow. This change will imperceptibly come about through practice, patience, perseverance and a trust in the Spirit within. It matters not if it takes weeks, months or years for this change to occur. It is the desire to change that is important. It is the desire and the focussed intention which will give us the drive and the courage to remain steadfast in our quest. It will come about. Our inner spirit is faithful and responsive to the inward and outward actions of our heart. Often other people notice a change within us.

We need to be conscious of the fruits of the Spirit or in particular one fruit of the Spirit in which we would like to grow. We need to keep this 'fruit' at the forefront of our mind. When we strive to be aware of the fruits of the Spirit in our lives we tend to become kinder, more peaceful, more patient or the like. As this happens something indefinable seems to change within us. Some would call this the work of the Spirit. Others may give it another name. All we know is that something begins changing within us and it is a good change. We may not initially notice this within ourselves. More often it is others who will comment. Accept the acknowledgement. But do not be distracted by it or become complacent. For us, it is enough to keep focussed on our 'becoming'.

'Chip away at the mountain and eventually the mountain will fall.'
(J Coleman, 1994)

For example, to become a person of kindness, most of us need to consciously and regularly practise acts of kindness. Eventually this fruit of the Spirit will take deeper root within our lives. We may practise a variety of acts of kindness. Taking the time to offer a smile often changes the disposition of the other and also of ourselves. Patience challenges many of us. We may have countless opportunities to practise the fruit of patience, such as waiting in a shopping line, at the traffic lights or a queue at the bank. Such opportunities to practise patience await us in many forms.

'By their fruits you shall know them...'   *(Mt 7: 20)*

Striving to grow in the nine fruits of the Spirit is a life-time adventure. They are gifts to all; be one a Christian or not. They are good values. They are the virtues of good people: Love, Peace, Joy, Kindness, Patience, Trustfulness, Self Control, Gentleness and Goodness.

CHAPTER THREE
Practice, Patience and Perseverance

Begin the journey!

We will already have grown naturally in some fruits of the Spirit. Identify this fruit (or these fruits) for yourself. Are you naturally a loving person, good or trustworthy? In contrast, which of the fruits is something of an 'Achilles heel'? For some it may be patience or others joy. This particular fruit may be a good place to start. Choose this fruit and deliberately begin to practise it each day. For many, this will demand conscious attempts to begin to change in order to become more patient or kind or more joyful. Write the 'fruit' on a card and put it in a prominent place. This often helps to prompt our memory. The reminder assists us to point our compass once again toward our goal.

What will be required of us? *Practice, Patience, Perseverance.* Strive to keep this fruit to the forefront of our mind. Seek ways to make it become a more natural part of our lifestyle or way of being. Enjoy the experience. In time, reap the benefits. We will become people who are more content and purposeful. This may not happen immediately. It is the tortoise, not the hare, who usually wins the race!

Focussing on a fruit of the Spirit is one way which concretely aids us to deepen our life in the Spirit or our life as people of the inner journey. We are people striving to live better lives. This is a simple yet purposeful way to guide our young. As a teacher, catechist or parent we have the privilege of breaking open the fruits of the Spirit to the young people in our lives.

In the book of Genesis we are told that each of us is made in the image of God (Genesis 1:26-27). Perhaps it may be said that the 'God spirit' is within each of us (whoever we are) drawing us into the fullness of 'who we are really meant to be'. This is an invitation offered to each of us. The response is our choice. With the guidance of the fruits of the Spirit we may respond more purposefully to life rather than drifting somewhat aimlessly like waves on the ocean. We can choose. The fruits of the Spirit are an ancient and true rudder that will guide us to the shore.

Confirmation:

At Confirmation the gifts that we received at our Baptism are simply sealed or confirmed. The closeness and relationship of these two sacraments is seen nowadays more easily when an adult is received into the Christian faith. The adult is baptised (or christened) then immediately signed with holy oil. This action signifies the confirming of what has just taken place at their baptism. We believe the Spirit is present with us the whole of our life from its very beginnings. The Spirit is present with us before our Confirmation if we receive this sacrament at a later age. How might we, then, begin to understand this 'Spirit within'?

A description of the 'Spirit within'

The Spirit (some say, 'Holy Spirit') may be described as the inexpressible love of the Father and the Son. How does one aptly portray what Christian's term 'the Trinity'? How can we begin to explain the Spirit (Holy Spirit) in terms understandable to our young? One way this amazing mystery may be described is by use of the following analogy.

A Way of looking at the Trinity

One way of considering this mystery of who or what the Spirit is, may be described through the following analogy:

A man's love for his wife and her love for him can be so strong that this love can bring forth new life. This being is a separate identity yet is of the father and the mother. This new life 'proceeds' from the husband's and wife's inexpressible mutual love.
Similarly, the great mystery of the Trinity may be expressed as follows: the love that the Father has for the Son and the Son for the Father is such that it defies words available to us. This mutual love, one for the other, is so powerful that it brings forth the Spirit. So the Spirit is separate; yet mysteriously, at the same time, one with the love

relationship of the Father and Son. In the Nicene-Constantinople creed (325 and 381 CE) the Catholic Church uses the word 'proceeds' to describe this mystery:

'We believe in the Holy Spirit, the Lord the Giver of life,
who proceeds from the Father and the Son'.

With this simple understanding of the great mystery of the Trinity within the Christian tradition, we may better appreciate how the 'Trinity or the Trinitarian mystery' lives within us. Appreciating more fully how the 'Spirit lives within us' may give us a clearer understanding of why growing in 'the fruits of the Spirit' is so important in our lives. Indeed, it is a challenge to fully live the fruits of the Spirit each day.

How patient are we really?

How kind are we to especially those people whom we do not particularly like?

How much self control do we have in all parts of our life?

However, like everything the desire to grow in the fruits of the Spirit has a beginning. The choice to begin this journey is always ours. Helping our young to appreciate this more and more is the privilege we have as teachers, catechists, parents or simply genuine seekers.

CHAPTER FOUR
The Nine fruit of the Spirit (Galatians 5:22)

Love
Love may be that which enables us to move beyond ourselves to desire what we might wish for another without expecting anything in return. Some describe it as something within us that draws us irresistibly to another while at the same time respecting them.

Peace
Peace may be described as a sense of being content. It may be seen in our speech and actions. We are not anxious or disturbed. Rather, it is an inner disposition which some may describe as contentment.

Joy
Joy some say is an inexpressible excitement that causes us to bring light-heartedness to ourselves and others in a variety of situations. We might say we are happy. Along with this may be a type of effervescence that overflows in our words and actions which may have a contagious effect. Similarly, one may feel a deeper sense of joy which is not as obviously effusive. Such a person still may be joyful but in a quieter way.

Kindness
Kindness might be found in the freely offered gesture which may benefit or assist the other. This action may be driven by our desire to do good for them whilst seeking no reward.

Patience
Patience could be described as having the ability to put aside our immediate wants and needs for another. We are willing to wait our turn even though we would like to have it now. We consider the needs of others when it is appropriate rather than immediately satisfying our own needs.

Trustfulness
Trustfulness may be seen as the ability to be diligent and loyal to both myself and to others. When something is entrusted to us, and we are at peace with this, we do not need to share it with others to gain their friendship or admiration. When we are given a responsibility we are reliable enough to see it through to its completion.

Self Control
Self control may be described as having the ability to wait or put off responding immediately. This could be particularly when it may be more prudent to wait, reflect and then respond; even though we may desire to act now! Delayed gratification may be one way of describing self control.

Gentleness
To be gentle could be described as having the inner strength to deal with another in a respectful manner. A person needs to be internally strong in order to be gentle. The truly gentle person is usually very strong internally. They have no need to dominate others. For example, the 'bully' at school is often a weak person (internally). 'Scratch' their rough exterior and one may find a person with fears lurking below. 'Bullies' appear to have a need to exert their power because internally they are usually vulnerable. To be truly gentle one needs to be internally strong. Sometimes it may be said that this person has insights into who they are and is able to accept themselves. The preeminent person of gentleness, many say, was Jesus, the Christ. He could be there for the weak yet responsibly challenge the strong!

Goodness
Perhaps this may be considered an ultimate fruit of the Spirit. For some, it captures and sums up all of the other fruits. To be truly a good person one needs to exhibit each of the other eight fruits of the Spirit.

CHAPTER FIVE
Let The Journey Begin!

The fruits of the Spirit help us develop a truth within and about ourselves. They offer a pathway and an end point to what some may call discovering and living our 'true self'. The fruits of the Spirit offer a principle for life. They are a simple yet profound blueprint for this journey. Some may call them guide-posts for life and at the same time they are like an end point to our striving to become fully who we are: content and at peace within and with our life. They do not leave us in complacency, but may be an impetus to our 'shalom'* – * 'that we may become the fullness of who we are meant to be'.

A growth in the fruits of the Spirit may be the result we see, in our lives, if we are striving to be better people. Learning to sit quietly or to have some 'thinking' time can help and act like a compass point to refocus us onto a 'good pathway'. Many would say it is the God-spirit within empowering us and guiding us towards being a better person; a person who is more at peace within.

Our growth in the fruits of the Spirit can lead us to an inner freedom. The fruits of the Spirit can aid us to become more open and receptive to others and their way of being. While we may not agree with their choices in life or their way of being, we are not threatened by 'who they are'. Indeed, the fruits of the Spirit assist us to become more understanding and compassionate towards the other.

Choosing one fruit of the Spirit as our goal and keeping this fruit at the fore-front of our mind each day will enable it to grow (in our lives). An approach to introducing the fruits of the Spirit is offered in the following chapter.

As a teacher, a catechist, parent or a genuine seeker it is important to affirm the efforts of our young ones. As Hebrews 3:13 states, 'Every day, as long as this 'today' lasts, keep encouraging one another...'

Begin the journey today! Enjoy the journey! Pathways of inner peace await us.

CHAPTER SIX
A Possible Introductory Timeframe

This is a suggested guide only
(Adapt usage to appropriate age level)

Day One: Make the nine fruits of the Spirit on cards (with the students/child)

Day Two: Make the tree and the sign such as:
'Ways we can be like Jesus'

Day Three: In about 10 minutes
a) hold up each fruit of the Spirit. The students name the fruit
b) then take 3 of the fruits of the Spirit. The students (in pairs) talk about what it means: i.e. they brainstorm together and then write how they might actually show this fruit of the Spirit in practical ways in the classroom, school or at home
c) students feedback these suggestions, in groups, to the teacher/catechist. Place their responses on a whiteboard or paper. Make a list of these suggestions. Leave the list until the next day.

Day Four: In about 10 minutes
a) cull the students' suggested list from the previous day until 3-4 points remain. Perhaps a democratic vote may be used
b) teacher copies these 3-4 points each onto separate strips
c) place the 3 or 4 strips of suggested ways (points) they can concretely live the fruits of the Spirit under its particular fruit of the Spirit near/under the 'Jesus Tree'.

Day Five: In about 10 minutes
a) take another 3 fruits of the Spirit. Invite the students to discuss what each fruit means and complete the task as in Day Three
b) feedback as a group to the teacher (who whiteboards their responses).

Day Six: In about 10 minutes
a) cull the students' suggestions to 3-4 points (from the previous day) for each different fruit of the Spirit. Again, a democratic vote may hasten the process. Teacher copies these responses onto a separate sheet as per Day Four.

Day Seven: In about 10 minutes
a) take the last 3 fruits of the Spirit. Again, invite the students to complete the process as per Day Three. Feedback in groups (whiteboard or paper).

Day Eight: In about 10 minutes
a) cull the students' suggestions to 3-4 points as per the Day Four
b) copy their responses onto separate strips and place them under the matching fruit under the 'Jesus Tree'.

Day Nine: In about 10 minutes
a) by now the students will have brainstormed the nine fruits of the Spirit and, with the teacher, will have selected 3-4 points (for each fruit of the Spirit) as ways they could actually live this out in the classroom, school or at home
b) students then select a fruit of the Spirit **as their primary goal**
c) they then select one point from this particular fruit of the Spirit as their goal to focus on for the next week (or however long the teacher/catechist decides is appropriate). This fruit and the way it could be lived out is then written onto their 'goal card' as a reminder of what they are striving to live each day
d) teacher/student writes: (use the 'Ways I may achieve this' sheet in the Appendix):

i) the fruit of the Spirit (the goal they have chosen to work on) is written in larger print

ii) underneath it is written the concrete way the student will strive to achieve this over the next period. (see point c above)

iii) the completed ('Ways I may achieve this') sheet is stapled into their RE book or work file or where their sheet will be stored

iv) the fruit of the Spirit and practical way of achieving this are both written onto their **small coloured Goal card which is velcroed** onto the student's desk. Using a non permanent pen enables this goal to be easily changed

v) this visual 'goal card' is used to affirm or remind the student of his/her chosen goal.

Day Ten: *Student/child conferencing* (this may need to be adapted to circumstances)
For about two minutes per student (or as appropriate – suggestion only) ask the student why they chose this particular fruit of the Spirit and how they intend to live it out. The goal card and 'Ways I may achieve this' sheet could be completed during this brief conference. This may be integrated as an assessment task for future reporting.

Day Eleven: Continue this interview process with each student.

Remember to praise the students who are meeting their goal.
Strive to encourage all students to meet their fruit of the Spirit goal.

CHAPTER SEVEN
Aids for the Journey

Some Classroom Ideas
(see appendix for further ideas)

1. *Fruit of the Spirit Bingo*
   - make a card (for each student) with various fruits of the Spirit placed randomly in each of the squares or rectangles
   - make numerous copies of each of the fruit of the Spirit to fit the squares or rectangles (enough for each class member to place onto the squares or rectangles as required for the game)
   - play bingo as one does in 'a Bingo game'. One may win with a top or side row covered
   - alternatively for a longer game; all squares or rectangles on the card may need to be covered to 'win' the game
   - if this game is being introduced to younger students; senior students of the school may be invited to produce the cards as a Numeracy and Literacy learning activity
   - such a game, for younger students may constitute a Literacy activity, Word recognition and/or Spelling activity.

2. *Fruit of the Spirit Story Books*
   - invite senior students to select one of the nine fruits of the Spirit and write a fictional story about this particular fruit, suitable for younger students
   - the student may choose the fruit of self control
   - these students then write about a situation, using a fictional character/s, who is challenged when having to use the fruit of self control
   - the story could be woven around this theme with a successful outcome
   - similarly, senior students may choose the fruit of patience. In the story the character may fail in a situation to display patience

- the character realises their failure and sets out to succeed on the next occasion
- the finished, illustrated books may be made available for younger students
- each senior student may be invited to share their story with a younger student.

3. *Fruit of the Spirit Chart*
   - the name of each student may be listed on a chart
   - students could acknowledge a fruit displayed by a peer by placing a 'fruit sticker' next to the student's name
   - these may be transferred to **a Portfolio record book** and/or a **Certificate** issued at the end of the week; fortnight or month.

4. *Fruit of the Spirit Booklet*
   - students may use their 'Booklet' to collect fruits of the Spirit stamps
   - make up a booklet with separate pages for each of the fruits of the Spirit
   - on each page is a set of squares. In each square, students receive a 'stamp' in recognition that they have shown this particular fruit in their behaviour
   - collecting a certain number of stamps may allow a student to receive an achievement award.

5. *Personal goal setting cards* (laminated Goal Cards)
   - these laminated Goal Cards may be used to remind students the fruit they wish to work towards achieving. (see Appendix)

6. *Fruit of the Spirit Nomination cards*
   - nominate others by filling in a form and place the nomination card into a suitable collection box
   - students nominating another in their class need to state the reason why they have chosen this student and the reason for choosing the particular fruit of the Spirit
   - each student may have a larger form to which they can add the sticker they received for this nominated fruit of the Spirit (add to their collection). They may display this on their desk or another suitable place.

7. *Sticker booklet and 'bowl'*
   - every time a student displays a particular fruit they may get a sticker to place onto the relevant page in their designed booklet
   - one fruit of the Spirit may be the focus per week
   - students collect their reusable laminated 'fruit' to add to their own personal fruit bowl/pouches.

8. *A Portfolio*
   - students may be given a certificate for displaying a particular fruit of the Spirit
   - this could be gained after receiving 5 or more nominations of a particular fruit
   - for example, each time a fruit of the Spirit is exhibited or noticed an 'x' may be placed next to their name on a displayed wall chart
   - this chart may be a way of tracking who has earned a certificate and used as a general celebratory or reporting tool.

9. *Fruit of the Spirit painting*
   - choose a gospel passage – e.g. Mark 4:26-29
   - students discuss what this passage might mean
   - they decide which fruit of the Spirit it might represent
   - students may draw the various elements represented in the passage
   - the finished art pieces could be presented to another class, displayed in the school library or congregational showcase area
   - one class may be ambitious enough to attempt a large piece of art work for the school or centre.

10. *Fruit of the Spirit Laminated windows*
   - each of the fruits of the Spirit may be displayed amidst coloured 'stain-glassed' cellophane paper.

APPENDIX

Some Activities (ideas) for Using the fruit of the Spirit

1. Write a letter naming a fruit of the Spirit which the student/child believes the local Bishop, Minister or Pastor exhibits. Pre-Literacy students may be encouraged to draw the fruit of the Spirit they have chosen. In many of the examples below Pre-Literacy pupils may illustrate their examples. An adult could transcribe their words.

2. Write on a card as a gift a fruit of the Spirit which the student/child believes a family member exhibits.

3. On a card write a fruit of the Spirit which the student/child believes the School Principal exhibits.

4. Choose a fruit of the Spirit for the chaplain which the student/child believes they exhibit.

5. Write on a card a fruit of the Spirit which the student/child believes a school staff, church or congregation member exhibits. Strive to include all members.

6. Write on a small card a fruit of the Spirit for ourselves – to carry in our pocket as a reminder of what we may be striving to develop for this week (or for a fortnight etc).

7. A fruit of the Spirit may be given to another member of the classroom home group – randomly selected (or arranged).

8. In groups of about 3, decide on 2 or 3 reasons that might hinder us from being people of _____ (choose a fruit of the Spirit). At the same time (or separately) what may be 2 or 3 ways (attitudes) we could adopt to become people of _____ (name the fruit of the Spirit for the week/fortnight)?

The hindrances and attitudes might be displayed within homeroom (secondary) as visual reminders. The students may accompany their work with designs that illustrate their work.

9. Develop large colourful paintings of each fruit of the Spirit.

10. Select an animal to represent a particular fruit of the Spirit. Draw or paint this. In a sentence (or two), state why you feel this animal represents a particular fruit of the Spirit.

11. Select something in nature to represent a particular fruit of the Spirit. Draw or paint this. In a sentence (or two) state why you feel this aspect of nature represents a particular fruit of the Spirit.

12. Offer a fruit of the Spirit card to a student they have noticed who may be 'doing it hard'.

13. Present a fruit of the Spirit card to a friend outside the homeroom group. This might mean that the student may have to explain what is being done in their homeroom group.

14. Which fruit is this? In groups, invite the students to write simple skits about each fruit of the Spirit. The actual fruit is not mentioned. The skits could be presented to others (particularly younger students in a school or church congregation) for them to decide which fruit of the Spirit is being displayed.

15. Invite early childhood students to talk about and/or illustrate their favourite fruit of the Spirit. Their transcribed words may be added to the illustration.

GOAL CARD
(photocopy and cut into three)

FRUIT OF:
GOAL:

FRUIT OF:
GOAL:

FRUIT OF:
GOAL:

WAYS I MAY ACHIEVE THIS

A possible Student Conference Sheet

Fruit of the Spirit	*Ways I May Achieve This*
Love	
Peace	
Joy	
Kindness	
	Ways I Could Improve
Patience	
Trustfulness	
Self Control	
Gentleness	
Goodness	

Student Goal	Comment:
Leader Goal	Comment:

Fruit of the Spirit	*Ways I May Achieve This*
Love	
Peace	
Joy	
Kindness	
	Ways I Could Improve
Patience	
Trustfulness	
Self Control	
Gentleness	
Goodness	

Student Goal	Comment:
Leader Goal	Comment:

The fruit of the Spirit

My name is ᵕᵕᵕᵕᵕᵕᵕᵕᵕᵕᵕᵕᵕᵕᵕᵕᵕᵕᵕᵕᵕᵕ

The fruit of the Spirit I am working to improve is

ᵕᵕᵕᵕᵕᵕᵕᵕᵕᵕᵕᵕᵕᵕᵕᵕᵕᵕᵕᵕᵕᵕᵕᵕᵕᵕᵕᵕᵕᵕᵕᵕᵕᵕᵕᵕᵕᵕ

ᵕᵕᵕᵕᵕᵕᵕᵕᵕᵕᵕᵕᵕᵕᵕᵕᵕᵕᵕᵕᵕᵕᵕᵕᵕᵕᵕᵕᵕᵕᵕᵕᵕᵕᵕᵕᵕᵕ

I can already do this by

ᵕᵕᵕᵕᵕᵕᵕᵕᵕᵕᵕᵕᵕᵕᵕᵕᵕᵕᵕᵕᵕᵕᵕᵕᵕᵕᵕᵕᵕᵕᵕᵕᵕᵕᵕᵕᵕᵕ

ᵕᵕᵕᵕᵕᵕᵕᵕᵕᵕᵕᵕᵕᵕᵕᵕᵕᵕᵕᵕᵕᵕᵕᵕᵕᵕᵕᵕᵕᵕᵕᵕᵕᵕᵕᵕᵕᵕ

I shall improve by

ᵕᵕᵕᵕᵕᵕᵕᵕᵕᵕᵕᵕᵕᵕᵕᵕᵕᵕᵕᵕᵕᵕᵕᵕᵕᵕᵕᵕᵕᵕᵕᵕᵕᵕᵕᵕᵕᵕ

ᵕᵕᵕᵕᵕᵕᵕᵕᵕᵕᵕᵕᵕᵕᵕᵕᵕᵕᵕᵕᵕᵕᵕᵕᵕᵕᵕᵕᵕᵕᵕᵕᵕᵕᵕᵕᵕᵕ

(for ECE students)

IMAGES OF THE FRUIT

Fruit of the Spirit

Love

Peace

Joy

Kindness

Patience

Trustfulness (Faithfulness)

Self Control

Gentleness (Humility)

Goodness

The fruit of the Spirit for everyday life!

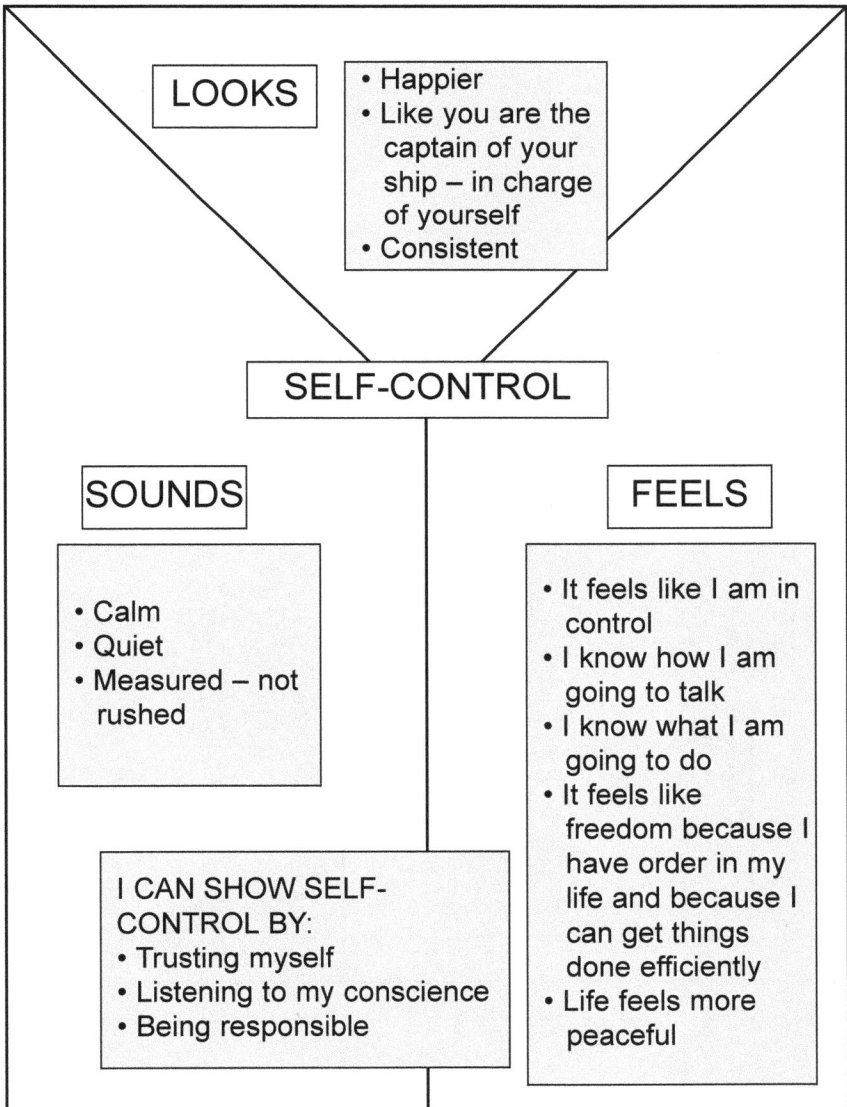

Y chart for fruit of the Spirit

(sample)

LOOKS
- Happier
- Like you are the captain of your ship – in charge of yourself
- Consistent

SELF-CONTROL

SOUNDS

- Calm
- Quiet
- Measured – not rushed

FEELS

- It feels like I am in control
- I know how I am going to talk
- I know what I am going to do
- It feels like freedom because I have order in my life and because I can get things done efficiently
- Life feels more peaceful

I CAN SHOW SELF-CONTROL BY:
- Trusting myself
- Listening to my conscience
- Being responsible

(template)

LOOKS

SOUNDS

FEELS

I CAN SHOW _____
BY:

The fruit of the Spirit for everyday life!

Blank Page

Comments by teachers on the fruit of the Spirit

My experience of using the Fruit of the Spirit in the classroom has far exceeded my initial thoughts and opinions. The possibilities this foundation offers to teachers and children are endless. It became apparent to me that through focusing on the Fruit of the Spirit, in all facets of my teaching, is such an influential and guiding tool, when one day a child put their hand up and told me ...
"Mr Love, It's like we are God's fruit bowl, and He doesn't want our fruit to be bruised. With these fruits we will always be ripe!"

B. Love – Teacher

The program allows the children to live their faith out in their daily lives. We focus each week on a fruit and set goals for ourselves to achieve this goal. When teaching about the Confirmation Sacrament, the children in our school have a deep understanding on the nine Fruit of the Spirit which is helpful when teaching about the Gifts of the Spirit.

L. Voss – Teacher

I found the Fruits of the Spirit session and ideas very useful. It provided a practical way to engage students to think more critically and consciously about the choices they make in their daily lives. We adopted a whole school approach with the information and both staff and students alike worked towards making more positive choices that reflected the work of the Holy Spirit.

C Walsh – Principal

I had a home group of 25 students (yrs 7-12) for 25 mins four days per week. A variety of strategies used from the fruit of the Spirit workshop helped refocus the students. This culminated in the whole group co-operating and producing a large painting based on Mark 4:26-29 (fruit-Patience). Student attitudes changed. I was truly grateful for the experience.

R Meder – Secondary Teacher

The presentation on the Fruit of The Spirit was superb and infectious. Not only did it inspire those already interested in the topic but it ignited great excitement and enthusiasm amongst the more skeptical members of the group. The presenter's variety of material, experience, anecdotes and suggestions on the Fruit of the Spirit were extremely helpful and very easy to understand and incorporate throughout the school for staff and students alike. A treasure chest was opened for us to explore and gather the priceless jewels within to not only share with others but use for our own lives too.

M Varley – Catechist, Children's author, Teacher Assistant

www.ingramcontent.com/pod-product-compliance
Lightning Source LLC
Chambersburg PA
CBHW060644030426

42337CB00018B/3444